1 Minuet メヌエット

W. A. Mozart
モーツァルト

2 March マ ー チ

W. A. Mozart
モーツァルト

3 Aria in F アリア ヘ長調

W. A. Mozart
モーツァルト

4 **Aria in D** アリア ニ長調

W. A. Mozart
モーツァルト

5 Slowly Ever Onward ド イ ツ 民 謡

Folk Song
ドイツ民謡

6 For He's a Jolly Good Fellow ド イ ツ 民 謡

Folk Song
ドイツ民謡

7 **Can You Count the Stars** ドイツ民謡

Folk Song
ドイツ民謡

8 **Within a Shady Valley** ドイツ民謡

Folk Song
ドイツ民謡

10

9 **Sleep, Darling Son** ドイツ民謡

C. M. v. Weber
ウェーバー

落付いたテンポで美しく歌う

Violin

Piano

10 **Down in the Lowlands** ドイツ民謡

Folk Song
ドイツ民謡

Allegretto

Violin

Allegretto

Piano

11 Drinking Song ドイツ民謡

Folk Song
ドイツ民謡

12 Coburger March コブルガーマーチ

German
ドイツ曲

13 Torgauer March トラガウェルマーチ

German
ドイツ曲

Part II

1 Aria in G アリア ト長調

W. A. Mozart
モーツァルト

2 **Allegro** アレグロ

W. A. Mozart
モーツァルト

3 Minuet メヌエット

W. A. Mozart
モーツァルト

4 Two Polonaises　2つのポロネーズ

W. A. Mozart
モーツァルト

I

Violin

Piano

Fine

Fine

II

I. Polonaise da Capo

I. Polonaise da Capo

23

5 Tyrolean Song ド イ ツ 民 謡

Folk Song
ドイツ民謡

6 Get Up, Merry Swiss Boy ド イ ツ 民 謡

Folk Song
ドイツ民謡

7 Pastorale 牧 歌

G. F. Handel
ヘンデル

8 Cradle Song 子守歌

W. A. Mozart
モーツァルト

9 Poor Orphan Child 哀れみなし児

R. Schumann
シューマン

10 Minuet メヌエット

L. van Beethoven
ベートーベン

Da Capo al Fine